THE LION'S SHARE
LA PART DU LION

English Animal Idioms
(French - English)
Expressions idiomatiques anglaises :
les animaux
(français - anglais)

By Troon Harrison
Illustrated by Dmitry Fedorov
French translation by Marine Rocamora

Language Lizard
Basking Ridge

For English audio and resources for teaching idioms, see the last page of this book.

The Lion's Share - English Animal Idioms (French-English)

Published by Language Lizard
Basking Ridge, NJ 07920
info@LanguageLizard.com

Visit us at www.LanguageLizard.com

First edition 2020

Library of Congress Control Number: 2020916954

ISBN: 978-1-951787-72-1 (Print)
ISBN: 978-1-951787-77-6 (Ebook)

WHAT IS AN IDIOM?

An idiom is a phrase that says one thing but means something different. An idiom can be a quick way of saying something complicated. Knowing idioms will help you to understand and speak English fluently. This book contains idioms about animals. *Note - The English idioms are translated* ***literally.***

QU'EST-CE QU'UNE EXPRESSION IDIOMATIQUE ?

Une expression idiomatique est une phrase qui possède une signification différente de son sens premier. Une expression idiomatique peut être un moyen de dire rapidement quelque chose de compliqué. Connaître ces expressions idiomatiques t'aidera à comprendre l'anglais et à le parler couramment. Ce livre contient des expressions idiomatiques en rapport avec les animaux. *Remarque : les expressions idiomatiques anglaises sont traduites* ***de manière littérale***.

ANTS IN YOUR PANTS
DES FOURMIS DANS TON PANTALON

Meaning: Not being able to stay still

Signification : ne pas être capable de rester en place

I can tell you are excited to see your grandmother because you have **ants in your pants.**

GETS MY GOAT

PRENDRE MA CHÈVRE

Meaning: Feeling annoyed

Signification : être agacé

It really **gets my goat** when my sister eats all the snacks.

BUSY AS A BEE
OCCUPÉ COMME UNE ABEILLE

Meaning: To work hard and quickly at a job

Signification : travailler vite et bien dans son travail

When Mom cleans the house, she is **busy as a bee**.

RAINING CATS AND DOGS

PLEUVOIR DES CHATS ET DES CHIENS

Meaning: Heavy rain that makes you very wet

Signification : une forte pluie qui te trempe

I forgot to bring my umbrella and now it is **raining cats and dogs**.

HOLD YOUR HORSES
TIENS TES CHEVAUX

Meaning: Be patient and don't be hasty

Signification : sois patient et ne te précipite pas

Hold your horses! You can join your friends after you finish your chores.

GET MY DUCKS IN A ROW
METTRE MES CANARDS EN RANG

Meaning: To be well prepared for something that is going to happen

Signification : être bien préparé pour quelque chose qui va arriver

Before moving to another country,
I had to **get my ducks in a row**.

BUTTERFLIES IN MY STOMACH
DES PAPILLONS DANS MON VENTRE

Meaning: Feeling nervous or excited

Signification : se sentir nerveux ou excité

When I sing on stage, I get **butterflies in my stomach**.

TAKE THE BULL BY THE HORNS
PRENDRE LE TAUREAU PAR LES CORNES

Meaning: Being brave, facing up to a challenge

Signification : être courageux, affronter un défi

I was scared to compete, but my coach told me to **take the bull by the horns**.

AS THE CROW FLIES
COMME LE CORBEAU VOLE

Meaning: The straight, direct route

Signification : la route droite, directe

The man thought it was not far to the valley as the crow flies.

UNTIL THE COWS COME HOME

JUSQU'À CE QUE LES VACHES RENTRENT À LA MAISON

Meaning: Doing something for a very long time

Signification : faire quelque chose pendant très longtemps

There is so much to sweep, I'll be working until the cows come home.

AT A SNAIL'S PACE
À UNE ALLURE D'ESCARGOT

Meaning: Doing something very slowly

Signification : faire quelque chose très lentement

When I'm late for school, Mom says I am moving **at a snail's pace.**

SMELL A RAT
SENTIR UN RAT

Meaning: Feeling that something is wrong

Signification : sentir que quelque chose ne va pas

A man said the bridge was safe, but I smelled a rat.

LET THE CAT OUT OF THE BAG

LAISSER LE CHAT SORTIR DU SAC

Meaning: Giving away a secret

Signification : révéler un secret

I wanted the party to be a surprise, but I accidentally **let the cat out of the bag.**

THE LION'S SHARE
LA PART DU LION

Meaning: Having the most of something

Signification : posséder la plus grande part de quelque chose

I tried to cut the pizza in half, but Dad told me to take **the lion's share**.

Visit www.LanguageLizard.com/Animal-Idioms for additional resources for teaching and learning English idioms, including:

- English audio of this book
- Multicultural lesson plans for use in the classroom or at home
- Information on the origin of the idioms in this book
- Additional animal idioms with their meaning, usage, and origin
- Information on idiom translations and idioms in other languages

This book is part of the **Language Lizard Idiom Series**.

Visit **www.LanguageLizard.com** for a complete listing of the titles in this series and available languages.

www.ingramcontent.com/pod-product-compliance
Ingram Content Group UK Ltd.
Pitfield, Milton Keynes, MK11 3LW, UK
UKHW062002290726
14090UKWH00021B/1340

9 781951 787721